Phone   808 222 9322

Powerstones

May 2011
Honolulu

Dearest Vi —
    It was a joy to have
had the pleasure of your
company there in Hawaii —
you are a grand and ebullient
spirit —
    So many Blessings to you
and your family —
        My Love and Aloha —
            Robin Stephens Rohr

Powerstones

LETTERS TO A GODDESS

AUTHORS
Linda Ching
Robin Stephens

First edtion 1994
Library of Congress Catalog
Card Number: 94-12045
ISBN: 0-9619891-4-9

Second edition 2004
Produced by Linda Ching and Robin Stephens Rohr

Printed in China

DESIGN BY LINDA CHING

To my parents
Stephen and Judy Ching
for empowering me with their beliefs.
Linda Ching

To Grandma Brooks
and
Thos Rohr
for their unrelenting love and support.
Robin Stephens

Contents

Preface

Each year more than 2,000 pounds of rocks are returned to Hawai'i Volcanoes National Park on the island of Hawai'i. Along with the rocks come thousands of letters. The letters are testimonials. They arrive from all over the world and are written in different languages by people who all claim to have experienced the same phenomenon: "Pele's curse."

For those unfamiliar with Hawaiian mythology, Pele is the volcano goddess. Hawai'i Volcanoes National Park is her sacred ground. Remove lava rock from the sacred ground, the legend goes, and a trail of bad luck will follow you.

Most of the people who visit Hawai'i Volcanoes National Park are tourists who take the rocks home as souvenirs. They do not believe in "Pele's curse." And then seemingly disastrous events befall them. So the rocks are returned with letters recounting the misfortune these people have experienced.

The returning of the rocks has been ongoing since the 1950s. As long-time Hawai'i residents, we had been aware of and fascinated by this story for years. But it wasn't until we read the letters during a visit to the park that we decided to collaborate on this book project.

Our original idea was to tell a simple yet intriguing story. The book would trace the mythological origins of the "curse" and present a sampling of the letters as evidence of the "curse's" apparent power. To provide the reader with a sense of place, the book would be illustrated with volcanic landscape photography, or "lavascapes" as we referred to them.

We began our research into the origins of "Pele's curse" at Honolulu's Bishop Museum. And what we uncovered startled us. According to Hawaiian scholars and educators, there was no evidence of or basis for the "curse" in Hawaiian mythology. What we later discovered was that in 1946 a park ranger, tired of visitors taking rocks as souvenirs, created the story of the "curse" as a way of discouraging the practice.

This surprising revelation forced us to rethink our premise. If the legend was a hoax, we asked ourselves, what was the point of the story that we were trying to tell? What we came to realize was that the real subject of our book is the power of beliefs.

We decided to expand the scope of our project to investigate how beliefs impinge upon our perception of the world and help create our reality. We chose to interview an international group of inspirational thinkers and achievers on this topic. We wanted to get their perspective on beliefs and the phenomenon of "Pele's curse." We also wanted to ask them how beliefs had shaped their own lives.

For the purposes of this book, these people have been divided into three categories: power thinkers, truth seekers and magic makers. Power thinkers are authors and philosophers who are grappling with new paradigms in the way human beings think about and interact with each other and the world. Truth seekers are people who are on a personal quest, very often religious or spiritual in nature, to solve life's deeper mysteries. Magic makers are actors, athletes, scientists and businesspeople who have achieved tremendous success in their fields and whose accomplishments uplift and inspire us.

Selecting the interviewees for this book and obtaining their consent was a formidable task. It was made even more difficult by the short six-month time frame we allowed ourselves to produce this work. But we decided that if this was truly going to be a book about the power of beliefs, part of the process should include creating a small "miracle" of our own. Thus, we came up with a wish list of people that we wanted to include and chose to believe that they would be interested and willing participants. We began writing letters and making phone calls. The response was tremendous.

And so what began as a commentary on a local cultural phenomenon became a book with a broader, universal appeal. The title Powerstones is, of course, a metaphor. It is a connecting link between the rocks that were the point of origin for this project and the interviewees who are its inspirational focus. These remarkable people, whose beliefs have empowered their own lives and the lives of people they come into contact with, are the true powerstones.

We would like to acknowledge the many people who wrote the letters that appear in the pages that follow. The letters run the gamut from comic to tragic. All are presented in the form that they were originally received. Only the names of the authors have been removed or changed to protect their privacy. We wish to emphasize that in publishing these letters we intend no disrespect and make no judgments about their content.

Lastly, we harbor the hope that this slim volume will help put an end to the taking of rocks from Hawai'i Volcanoes National Park. The practice is not only illegal, it is a form of environmental desecration. Above all else, this book is a love letter to a very sacred ground. May we keep it intact and may it inspire generations to come.

— *Robin Stephens and Linda Ching*

Introduction

Scholars and skeptics have long insisted that the myths we live by are human artifacts, deliberately fashioned to teach a moral lesson by telling a story that is, by turns, frightening, consoling, and edifying. As plausible as this suggestion may be, the idea that myths are designed to serve mundane human purposes rather than divine ones has always had an element of surmise or conjecture about it. This is because the origins of most myths are lost to us in a misty and anonymous past, with no mere mortal on whom to hang authorship.

This volume lays out the fascinating story of one distinctly contemporary myth—yet one that is no less intriguing or less powerful for its recent origins. We see here the story of Madame Pele's Curse from beginning to end. We learn how it originated, how quickly it took hold and, above all, how intently ordinary people have accepted its narrative thread as a string to make sense of their lives and their fate. What we grasp here is both how mundane and ordinary the roots of myth-making can be and how, despite their prosaic origins, they can quickly acquire both credibility and potency.

The general outlines of the author's tale are easy to sketch: in the 1950s a Big Island tour guide—perhaps impatient with returning tourists filling up his bus with rocks and sand—concocts a story: the goddess of the volcano, Madame Pele, puts a curse on anyone who removes her "children." Soon, other tour guides repeat the story, doubtless embellishing it in the re-telling. Tourists to the islands, cynical about "primitive" folkways, smile indulgently at the story while they continue scavenging for souvenirs and hauling them back home.

Years later, some of those same tourists find their lives in tatters. Faced with the loss of a job, the death of a loved one, a debilitating disease, or a nasty divorce, they cast about for some explanation of their fate. Perhaps while rummaging through memorabilia in the bottom of a closet or at the back of a drawer, they find the purloined lump of lava from Hawai'i. They remember the curse. Click! Everything falls into place: all their recent bad fortune stemmed from this one small act of sacrilege. How to put things right? Well, obviously, return the stuff whence it came.

This story, or some variant of it, has been repeated thousands of times in the last few decades, as the huge mounds of returned stones outside the ranger's station at Hawai'i Volcanoes National Park attest. More detailed testimony comes from the poignant letters excerpted here, replete with tragi-comic rehashings of all the ills that have befallen some of those who have removed the rocks from their natural resting place.

Confronted with so many people whose lives clearly took a turn for the worse after they pinched a small rock or a handful of sand, what are we to make of the curse? Should we suppose that there really is something to it? There are several possible avenues to pursue. One idea might be that the curse is literally true. What we know about the decidedly non-sacred circumstances of its concoction makes that an implausible alternative. Tour guides, after all, are scarcely the cultivators of ancient wisdom. But perhaps, even granting the myth's mundane origins, the curse becomes real for those who believe it. That is not so compelling either, as soon as one realizes that most of those who suffered long runs of bad luck were not initial believers. As they see it now, realization of the authenticity of the curse has been forced upon them by events, not by their prior disposition. (Indeed, had they credited the curse to begin with, they presumably would never have tempted fate by removing the rocks in the first place.) No, the authors of these letters are latter-day converts, not original believers; they are persons whose lives have entered downward spirals and whose change of fate is offered as vivid testimony to the power and the reality of the previously disbelieved curse.

What are we to make of these stories, we who are not caught up in the transgression? The famous English philosopher, Sir Francis Bacon, faced a similar conundrum almost four centuries ago. Known to be leery about the power of prayer, he was taken to the English sea coast to visit a Christian chapel for sailors. Its walls were bedecked with sketches of mariners who, having prayed for a safe voyage, had later been ship-wrecked and survived. In appreciation, they sent drawings of themselves back to the small chapel. To a man, they credited their survival to the prayers they offered before setting sail. The local chaplain obviously hoped to impress upon Bacon the efficacy of thus petitioning the Almighty. Bacon's response was telling: Where, he wanted to know, were the portraits of all the seamen who, having offered up their prayers in the chapel, subsequently perished at sea?

The parallel with our Pele curse is clear. What the collection of visitor letters at Hawai'i Volcanoes National Park shows is that, among the tens of millions of tourists who have probably taken home small chunks of the Big Island, a few thousand lived to regret it. The overwhelming majority who stole from Madame Pele presumably are, so far as we know, none the worse for having done so; at least they have taken no steps to make amends, and one supposes in those circumstances that they do not judge their fate as being much worse than that of the ordinary person. Indeed, there may be as many good luck stories enjoyed by those who took rocks away as there are bad luck stories. But, of course, the people whose lives have changed for the better are not going to be returning rock to Volcanoes park rangers, nor writing plaintive letters begging that the curse be undone. Like the drawings in Bacon's chapel, this collection of letters about the curse is thus inevitably slanted so as to reveal but one side of the story. But what an intriguing side it is!

Larry Laudan, PhD
Professor of Philosophy
University of Hawai'i

*An astonishing number of letters
are sent to Volcanoes National Park
each year testifying to the powers of
Pele's rocks. Whether this growing
belief is based on fiction or fact,
they give us cause to ponder.*

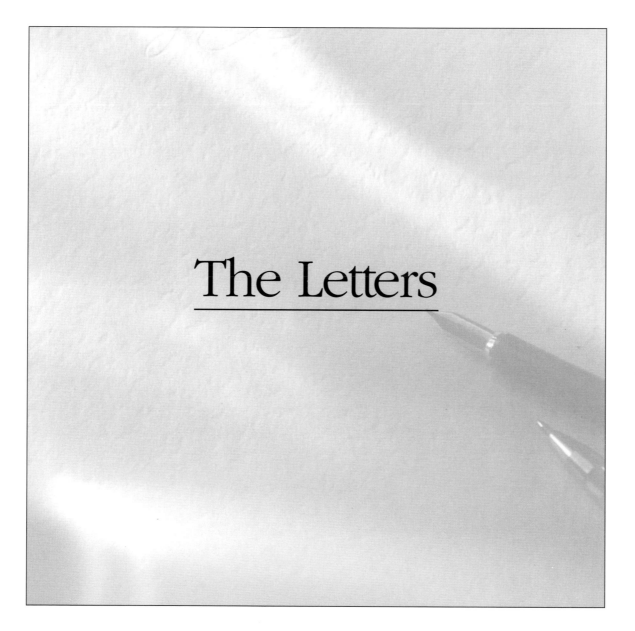

The Letters

THESE BELONG TO:

MME PELE

PLEASE RETURN —
ENOUGH IS ENOUGH !

Dear "Madam Pele,"

Sorry we took these 19 years ago to remember our vacation by. We just found out they are 2 of your children. I hope you recognize them and are happy to see them back again! We didn't know we were "kidnapping" your "Kids!"

Dear Sir

Please return the rock to the park. I'm not superstitious but I have no doubt __

The Curse Works

Dear Sirs,

I am returning 2 samples of lava rock from the Volcanoes National Park. I took them to demonstrate to my classes.

Since doing so I have been in an auto accident, taken 2 severe falls, had my basement flooded and spent numerous hours in doctors' offices for treatment. Currently my hand is numb and has been so for weeks.

I am no longer dubious about Pele's powers.

Please return these rocks for me to the volcanic area with my deepest apologies.

Sincerely,

To Whom It May Concern: (Pele)

Please return the contents of this box to the trail going to

to ocean and to the black sand beach. HURRY!!!!!!!!!!!!!!!!!!

Dear Sir:

Please return the enclosed lava rock to the place where it rightfully belongs, on the island of Hawaii.

I took this rock when I visited Hawaii in October 1974. A few months later I met the man who I eventually married. For the past 16 years this man has made my life miserable. I am truly sorry for taking the lava rock and I would like for it to be returned to its place of origin.

Thank your for your help.

Sincerely,

Dear Park Rangers

.This piece of lava came
into my possession from a
friend who visited the
Islands.

My Stepmother who,
I now live with, and is
a native Hawaiian will not
let this piece of lava stay
in this house for more than
24 hours. She says to please
return this to Madam Pele,
with all do respect.

We won the $600,000
lottery — we would
have won the
$2,000,000 one if it
wasn't for this —
please take the
rocket back before
more bad luck.

July 24, 1993

Dear Park Suc,

Please accept the return of black sand from black sand beach near Kilaeau Volcano. While visiting 3 years ago I remember that taking Pélé would bring me bad luck, so I figured black sand down the coast would bring only a little bad luck   I return her to you — even a little bad luck is not needed   I have lost 2 girlfriends and my grandmother in the last 3 yrs.   It is unfortunate that Pélé did not enjoy her time in the MIDWEST.

Most humbly,

32

Dear mr. Park Ranger my
my grandpa accidently took a Lava Rock
Because He dideht Know it was Bad Luck.

Love Mary Anne

In July 1973, while visiting the Uwekahuna or Halemaumau area of Kilauea Crater I picked up this rock after I was told not to. When I returned home I went through a messy divorce. Since then I've had innumerable problems. I nearly lost my job due to depression, I developed a very rare bone disease, have had several strokes, have lost part of my sight, have had several operations and finally had to take an early retirement due to my disabilities. Recently my bone disease has turned into Leukemia and I'm being treated on a week to week basis. I have a 50/50 chance of going into remission. Although I don't believe in the Polynesian Gods or their legions, I'm not in a position to argue so I'm returning the rock that I took along with my apologies.

Other than the above I enjoyed my visit to your islands.

Dear Pele,

All right I am convinced. I visited Hawaii in 1987 and during my stay absconded with some of your precious volcanic black sand. I am sorry, humbly apologize and vow never to do so again. I did this in spite of the many dire warnings given to me and since that foolish act have suffered many negative experiences ranging from the near collapse of my business to lesser but equally traumatic problems. <u>Lighten up Pele</u>, I think I've suffered enough. It was not until I recalled that I had this illicit pile of sand that I realized it had to be you behind the scenes stage managing one unhappy experience after another just for me. I have learned my lesson and vow complete obedience to your impressive power and reach.

Dear Sirs:

Please give the enclosed black sand back to Pele. It is still in the original container in which I removed it from the beach.

My husband and I went to Hawaii on our honeymoon in April/May of 1989. Our guide told us that it is bad luck to take the black sand, however, not being superstitious, I took some. My husband advised against it, but I'm stubborn and I took it anyway.

In the last three years, the following has happened:

1.   The battery was stolen from of our Toyota.
2.   The Toyota was stolen
3.   Our brand new car (Grand Am) was hit.
4.   My husbands father was put in the hospital due to passing out for no apparent reason (they still don't know what happened)
5.   My brother-in-law lost his job.
6.   My sister lost her job.
7.   I badly strained my back.
8.   Our Grand Am was stolen, found badly damaged but repairable.
9.   My mother had a mastectomy.
10.   My husband got sick, had tests, and it was determined he was exposed to TB (he only has the virus in his system, not the disease) and now has to be on medication for 9 months.
11.   My sister-in-law was diagnosed with Multiple Sclerosis.
12.   Our Grand Am was stolen again

I am now asking Pele for forgiveness. I will never doubt a superstition again, and the next time I am advised against doing something, believe me, I will not do it.

Thank you very much for listening to my tale of woe and accepting the black sand back.

RE: RETURN OF LAVA ROCK & PUMPICE GRAVEL

OBJECT: TO LIFT THE CURSE....

DEAR MADAME PELE:

ENCLOSED PLEASE FIND SOME LAVA THAT MY HUSBAND AND
I TOOK HOME AS A SOUVENIOR IN 1973 FROM A LAVA
FLOW THAT CLOSED THE BLACK SAND BEACHES.

WE DIDN'T REALIZE IT WAS TABOO (BAD LUCK) TO KEEP
LAVA, AND THAT IT WOULD MAKE YOU ANGRY.

WE CERTAINLY HAVE HAD MORE THAN OUR SHARE OF BAD
LUCK, AND WE ARE TERRIBLY SORRY TO HAVE ANGERED
YOU.
PLEASE ACCEPT THESE BACK, WITH OUR MOST HUMBLE
APOLOGIES, AND **PLEASE RELEASE THE CURSE.**

Dear Park Staff Personnel

Sorry to subject you to more lava—
people won't leave me alone—they keep
telling me to send it back— I dunno—
maybe there are spirits, maybe, I dunno—

DEAR VOLCANO NATIONAL PARK,

WHEN I WAS IN JUNIOR HIGH SCHOOL MY FATHER VISITED HAWAII AND BROUGHT THIS ROCK BACK TO ME. SINCE THEN IT'S POSSIBLE THAT IVE BEEN HAVING MUCH BAD LUCK EVEN THOUGH I DIDN'T TAKE IT MYSELF. IN EITHER CASE I HAVE SINCE GONE TO COLLEGE AT U.C. DAVIS AND HAVE LEARNED ABOUT TAKING THINGS FROM THEIR HOMES. BEING ENVIRONMENTALLY CONCIOUS I HAVE NEVER LOST SIGHT OF THE ROCK IN HOPES THAT ONE DAY I WOULD BE ABLE TO RETURN IT PERSONALLY WHEN VISITING YOUR FINE ISLAND AND PARK. UNFORTUNATELY CALIFORNIA HAS BEEN HIT PRETTY HARD BY THE RECESSION AND THAT TRIP SEEMS A LONG WAY OFF. I WOULD APPRE-CIATE IT IF YOU WOULD RETURN MY ROCK TO HER PROPER PLACE. I THINK SHE MISSES HER HOME. I WISH I COULD TELL YOU WHICH PARK IT CAME FROM BUT LIKE I MENTIONED, MY DAD TOOK IT AND I'M NOT TOO FAMILIAR WITH THE ISLANDS. I HOPE YOU'LL KNOW WHAT

TO DO. COULD YOU DO ME A FAVOR AND LET ME KNOW WHAT HAPPENS TO MY ROCK? WILL I STILL BE CURSED IF IT GOES TO THE WRONG ISLAND? THE ROCK HAS BEEN A PART OF MY LIFE SINCE I WAS ABOUT 13. (I AM NOW 26) I WOULD ALSO LIKE TO KNOW THAT SHE MADE IT SAFE BACK TO THE ISLANDS. IF YOU SEND A NOTE BACK I WILL BE FOREVER GRATEFUL. PLEASE ACCEPT THIS $10 DONATION TO THE PARK. IT'S NOT MUCH BUT IF I MAKE IT OUT TO HAWAII, I'LL BE GLAD TO BUY WHOEVER TAKES CARE OF THE ROCK A BEER OR SODA. I AM A REAL ESTATE AGENT AND UPON THE CLOSING OF MY NEXT SALE I'M MAKING PLANS TO VISIT MY FRIEND WHO LIVES ON OAHU SO I'LL STOP BY. ANYWAY, THANKS FOR HELPING ME OUT. ALOHA!

P.S I SAVED THE ROCK ABOUT 3 TIMES WHEN VARIOUS FAMILY MEMBERS AND GIRLFRIENDS TRIED TO THROW IT OUT!

Well to make a long story short, I did take lava rocks and black sand back home with me. And, believe it or not I have felt her anger ever since. So I beg you to somehow relieve me of my guilt by doing me the greatest favor on earth by returning to the Goddess Pele what rightly belongs to her, ----- the enclosed LAVA ROCKS AND BLACK SAND.

Before becoming too old to travel, it is my fondest hope to make one more trip to your lovely HAWAII, at which time I hope to stop in and thank you personally for making it right for me with Goddess Pele.

Forever grateful,
NO NAME PLEASE
name and address shown on package are fictious.

Dear Sirs:

I have sent you this package of lava rock and sand so that you might do me a favor and give it back to Pele. I have heard for years that taking Peles' lava rock from the islands was bad luck but didn't believe it. In 1989 my folks went to the islands and brought me back this "souvenir." Since that rock has been in my home, I have had unbelievably bad luck, including the death of my best friend at the hand of an intruder. There's probably nothing to the old superstition, but hey, I'm not taking any chances. Please give the lava back to Pele, with my regards. I'll settle for good ol' chunks of Ks. limestone or quartz pebbles from Colorado streams.

Thank you

Dear Madame Pele,

Up until now I haven't been a very superstitious person. I'd walk under ladders, step on cracks in the sidewalk, and laughed at black cats crossing my path.

My husband, two daughters and I were guests of your wonderful state in 1987. We visited Oahu and the Big Island. On Hawaii we got to see a black sand beach. Of course we <u>had</u> to take some of the sand home as a souvenir, even though we were cautioned not to because it wasn't safe to take lava off the island.

Madame Pele's curse was just another superstition to be set aside and forgotten. Or so we thought.

Enclosed is all of the black sand and lava that we brought back that year. We have had nothing but bad things happen to us since we brought it home.

One example is our oldest daughter had an accident and broke her back in 1989. She is fine now and is married with two children. There have been tragic incidents like this every year, so we believe we better return Pele's lava to it's home.

So, Madame Pele, please accept this as an apology and when we return next year to your beautiful state we will honor your wishes.

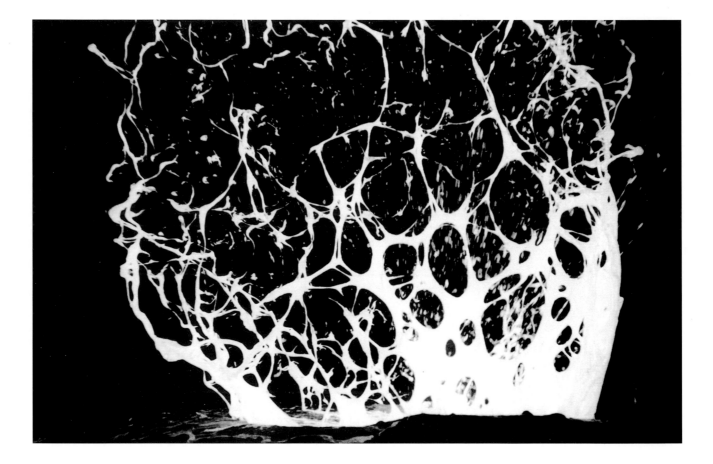

Dear Pele:

    During a trip to the big island in 1988 I removed some
black sand from a beach. I didn't make the connection at
the time between the black sand and the fact that it is
really lava which has been broken down by the action of
waves.

    Before this happened, I had been having a meteoric rise
in my career and everything in general was going well in my
life. Shortly after my return from Hawaii I was the victim
of a case of bad luck which caused me by sheer chance to be
present at the scene of major event which has ruined my
career. As a result of media pressure, I was made a scape-
goat for the actions of many of my subordinates. My employers
could not or would not withstand the pressure to render up a
"villain" upon whom the blame was to fall and when the
New York Times editorialized against me personally, the axe
fell on me. Although I was not fired, I was banished to a
career backwater in which I still linger, almost four years
later. I was told at the time "Just keep your mouth shut
about this because everyone (in my organization) knows you
didn't do anything wrong. In a few months they'll resurrect
you and have to take care of you because they'll owe you for
being a 'good soldier'." All this time has passed and nothing
has been done to correct the wrong done to me.

    Since 1988 I have had other instances which make me
wonder why all this is happening. For example, I've had my
car stolen, I've had my insurance cancelled and was barely
able to replace it. I went into the hospital for a routine
surgical procedure and nearly died from the resulting infec-
tion.

    I've had it. I don't really believe in the supernatural
but this has gone too far and too many people have told me to
get rid of the black sand. You win. Here it is. Now leave
me alone.

Enclosed are lava pieces that I picked up on my vacation in
Hawaii in 1991. Since that time my family has had
unbelievable bad luck. We have visited Hawaii many times
and have never brought back any lava. However on this
particular trip we did and now I'd like to return it.

Since then:

(1) my mother was operated on for lung cancer.

(2) I inherited my dad's mobile home when he passed away in
1990, and have not been able to sell it (and I can't rent it
out because of rules in the mobile home park).

(3) My oldest son: got divorced, got in a motorcycle
accident, and went to prison (all within a 6 month period).

(4) My husband had a brain hemorrhage, and 2 months later
had to undergo brain surgery at a hospital 300 miles from our
home.

(5) The day we got back from the hospital the pipes broke
under our kitchen floor which is a concrete slab, and flooded
our living room, dining room and kitchen.

(6) I developed angina, and a rapid heart rate and have to
take medication now.

(7) My only brother is not speaking to me. We have never
had an argument or fight in our lives.

(8) My collie dog that I've had for 11 years died.

(9) My 5 year old grandson broke his right arm at day-care
and two weeks after the cast was off, broke his other arm.

(10) I have just recovered from gall bladder surgery.

(11) My husband is still not working and I found out about 2
months ago that my job may be closing down at the end of the
year.

These are the major things that have happened in our family.

Dear Park Service Employees,

When I was on the Big Island in October I asked a Park Ranger where I might find some black sand to show my students at the high school where I am a science teacher. I was instructed to go to Kalapana Beach. I gathered Sand and as you can see I gathered lava to fill out the exhibit on volcanoes. Also a lady in the office behind the museum gave me some magazines to further illustrate volcanoes. The response from students was great. After having the exhibit in my classroom for a week I moved it to a display case in the hall of the science department where it was visible to all of our student body of 650 as they were on their way to their science classes.

At this point I am essentially through with the exhibit. Rather than store it in a closet I feel it is best to return the exhibit to you in order that you may loan it to other teachers when they come through the Park. This way they may also share what they have seen and learned about volcanoes with their students. I am doing this partly to set my friends at ease as they truly believe in the legend of Pele and are seriously worried for my well being. At the very least the legend of Pele puts in the proper perspective of sharing rather than taking only for our personal use. The lesson here is stewardship of the earth's resources and science teachers must be preaching this if we are to survive.

Dear Park manager:

Your information & warnings are correct! This piece of Pile's hair is being returned with the hope that she will forgive us for taking it from it's homeland. We have had many very serious things happen to us since taking this little "souvenir" in July of 1991 ... so serious that my husband & I almost made the worst mistake of our life - to get a divorce. If you knew us, you would know that this could not happen under any other circumstance!

Dear Superintendent Judd,

I am in great need of your assistance. I have inadvertently gotten into a situation that needs to be corrected, and I desperately need relief.

My problems began on June 12, 1990. A few days before this, my family and I began our long anticipated vacation in your beautiful state. A portion of this vacation was a trip to see the volcano Kilauea. As active volcanoes in Florida would have to be considered rare, we were all very excited about seeing an active volcano. When we arrived at the part of Route 11 were the lava had flowed across the road on it's way to the sea, the spectacle was all we had expected and considerably more. There at the side of the road, I saw the numerous offerings to Pele, and thought how wonderfully quaint. I must confess, in my ignorant state, I had very little respect for the power of Pele at that time.

As I wanted to have a momento of this wonderful experience, I selected a small piece of lava rock. I brought this home with me and proudly displayed it on my desk at the office.

Recently, I have been told that Pele does not permit the removal of her work, and that a very unpleasant price is exacted from those who do. I can attest to this from personal experience. The price has been unpleasant indeed. My business has had terrible results almost from the day I took this souvenir. Terrible is really an understatement. Unbelievable would be much more accurate.

I have been assured this affliction of bad luck will disappear only when Pele's volcanic rock is returned. I, and a large number of my fellow workers, would be very grateful if you would return the enclosed to it's proper place. I would be pleased to do this myself, but business misfortune usually has financial consequences. Therefore, a trip to do this myself is impossible. Candidly, I am pleased to have the money to buy a stamp.

If a virgin sacrifice would be helpful, please advise specifying gender preference. As you are perhaps aware, people who would qualify for this are not as plentiful now as they used to be. With that in mind, I will start the search now for a proper candidate, in case this is needed.

Volcanoes National Park
Hawaii Hawaii 96718-0053

Sir I am returning the Black Sand
which I took from the Black
Sand beach at Punaluu in
1980 when my husband and I
visited the Big Island.
As you can guess this sand
has brought me a great deal
of bad luck and hard times
the final blow come when my
husband took his life —

Sincerely

Hawaii Volcanoes National Park –

Almost 20 yrs. ago, I took home a
piece of rock from the volcano as
a souvenir of paradise. After learning
the legend that Pele bestows bad
luck, I'm returning the rock
to its original home.
I've been quite fortunate
over the years – except for
a few broken hearts –
but perhaps by returning
this to Pele, I'll find
my true love.

Mahalo,

To Whom It May Concern,

In August of 1989 my family and I had the wonderful experience of visiting your breathtaking park and island. We had the privilege of seeing first hand what an active volcano can do. During the tour, we, like many other mainland tourists took an inexpensive souvenir, some of the lava from the lava beds in your park. Our tour guide warned us that removing any materials was against the law, but worse, would bring "bad luck" to those who didn't heed the warning. We are not superstitious people. Upon returning to the mainland and returning to his job of 8 years, my husband was "let go" from his job and has been unable to find a job since. I am returning this small sample of lava to you. Please toss it as far as you can back into the lava fields, where it rightfully belongs and should stay. I am asking for your forgiveness. From now on, pictures and memories will be all we ever take from a wonderful and beautiful display of nature's work.

A Letter to Pele

This last February when I was in Hawaii, I foolishly took rocks from your mountains and caves.

I'd like to say I only took them for souvenirs.... but that isn't true. The main reason I took them was to prove I didn't believe, in you and the superstition.

Well, Pele.... I get the message.... finally too much has happened to me and my family.

I've fought it all along, but now I give up. Here are the rocks. I return them with humility. I sincerley apologize for playing rebellious games with things I didn't understand. I am so sorry.

I thought the wrath of Pele was just another _historical_ way of putting women down.

I've gained much more respect for the spirit world.

thanx for teaching me.

Dear Sir or Madam,

Enclosed you will find what has become the biggest

mistake we ever made. We ask the Goddess Pele for

forgiveness, to forgive our arrogance in thinking

we could hold her raw, chaotic, elemental power. We

ask that peace and harmony be restored to our lives

in returning these to her.

       Sincerely,

Dear Volcano National Park,

Please return Pele's children to her with our gift. My mother scooped up these rocks just seconds after the ranger gave the lecture on why not to take them. Normally a law abiding citizen, her brains must have been elsewhere. In the last month, we have had an auto accident, our house is broken into and our plane crashed on landing in Dallas! We have heard enough strange but true stories about people who steal bits and pieces from parks and how Madam Pele does not appreciate being flung about by infidels. I am returning this lava as my family and I are to moving to Hawaii (tomorrow) and I do not want to take any chances of irritating you know who.

P.S. I can't believe I'm writing this.

Goddess Pele,

I am returning your black sand. I found it in my closet as I cleaned it out during divorce. We got it in Nov. 1983 just before marrying. The entire marriage was a disaster. It ended with my husband going to jail for molesting our daughter this year. As part of my healing process, it feels much lighter & freer to be returning this black sand to its rightful place.

Enjoy!

Dear Madame Pele —

I am returning your Lava Rocks. I was told I
could take them, if I dared - and I did - I'm sorry.
I believe Madame Pele is a powerful spirit - and does
not want her handiwork disturbed by intruders to
the Island.
Since I brought these Rocks home—
1) My husband was run over by his own Truck - which
then crashed into a house.
2) My cataract surgery was a total failure - followed by
more surgery that failed.
3) My Mom developed Cancer and died (all with in 5 weeks).
4) I used these Rocks as decorations at a friend's Birthday
Party he died 4 weeks later.
5) I inherited my Moms house - I have lost many

thousands of dollars fixing it up to sell – and can't sell it – am going through foreclosure.

6. I have lost 9 other friends and relatives since my visit to Hawaii – through death.

7. Have gone through a divorce.

8. My income has dropped to 1/3 of what it was.

9. Surgeries – Hospitals, etc. have driven me to the edge of Bankrupsie

10. Leans have been put against my home

11. Pipes broke in my house and my Mom's doing extensive damage. No reason for the breaks.

12. One car has been obliterated in an accident. The other went dead in the driveway – to the tune of $500 for Towing and to get it to run again.

These are just some of the things that have happened. Yes, I believe in Madam Pele's Power.

Dear Madam Pele,

I am returning these lava rocks to your home with my regrets for having taken them. Please restore me to your good graces. I can not mentally, physically or emotionally go through any more bad luck. I know in my heart that you Madam Pele, the Great Fire Goddess, should always be respected and looked upon for your powers and beauty, and that every part of your wonders remain in its place. Once again, I ask for your complete forgiveness.

Respectfully yours,

Very sorry Madame Pele! It's true. It is so true! I have had nothing but stress and tragedy in my life since we left Hawaii in 1988 with this lava! Seriously -- I was warned about not taking lava by my parents who were stationed on Oahu in 1953 -- My innocent mistake was thinking they meant from Volcanoes National Park as I thought that was Pele's domain. Then upon returning to the States, I was told all of the lava is hers. I won't bore you with the details. I am not a superstitious person, but we landed in New York City the moment the World Trade Center blew up. That has been a metaphor for my life ever since. Jobs, relationships, health, all disintegrating. The timing is all too mysterious. I WANT MY HAPPY LIFE BACK.

Hawaiian Volcano State Park

I am returning these rocks, along with this brief explanation in hopes others hear & _listen_.

My husband and I came to Hawaii in July 1988 (his first visit). We took the rocks, even after hearing the legend.

We separated in August 1989. In May 1990 he was diagnosed with lung cancer — the tumor the size of a football. My husband had been a very healthy man all his life. Mike died of cancer November 2, 1990.

When I cleaned his house last week. I found these rocks — I am returning them to where they belong.

I hope others listen. I wish Mike would have listened.

Dear Park Rangers Big Island,

Please accept these pieces of volcanic rock back in the
hopes that Pele will be appeased and cease to curse the two
members of my ex-wife's family who love the Hawaiian Islands
the most.
I believe that my ex-wife's father took these rocks
from the Big Island sometime during the 1980's. At that
time, he was a vice-president of a company that specialized
in building banks. He owned a 400,000 dollar house, drove a
Cadillac, had a ski boat, many other toys, and a wonderful
family.
Since the late 1980's he has gone bankrupt, lost his
house, his job, most of his other toys, and is now living in
a rented house the rent which is paid by his son. He has no
money and struggles everyday to rebuild his life.
Approximately three and a half years ago, my wife and I
moved to Washington. I believe that in the process of that
move, this box of rocks got up mixed up with our belongings
and was stored in our garage since then. It appears that
some of Pele's wrath has been directed to us.
Since we acquired the rocks our lives have been
unhappy. My ex-wife began to be very unhappy, decided she
wanted to live independently and divorced me. We were
forced to sell our house. My ex-wife now lives in another

town, is struggling to make ends meet -- and is still unhappy.

I have only been to the Hawaiian Islands once. That trip was made with my ex-wife -- who I still love very much -- and is one of the most memorable ten day periods in my life. Of all the places we saw in the Island, my favorite place was on the volcanoes of Hawaii. I will never forget the legend of Pele and all the letters from people who had been foolish enough to take the rocks away from Pele.

I was shocked when we were moving out of our house and I found these rocks. I COULDN'T BELIEVE THAT MY FORMER FATHER-IN-LAW -- A MAN WHO I KNOW LOVES THE HAWAIIAN ISLANDS -- WOULD HAVE BEEN CRAZY ENOUGH TO TAKE THESE ROCKS OFF THE ISLAND!

Please give these rocks back to Pele with my apologies. It is my sincere wish that she will then cease to apply her curse on my ex-wife's family and allow them and me to live happily.

And finally, to all of you who may read this letter and think that this legend of the Goddess of Fire is not true -- BEWARE! Enjoy the splendor of Hawaii while you are there and don't carry home anything but some great memories and maybe some pictures.

The belief in the power
of stones is as ancient
as it is universal.

He Ola Ka Pōhaku

There is life in the stone and death in the stone

Old Hawaiian proverb

He Ola Ka Pōhaku

There is life in the stone and death in the stone
Old Hawaiian Proverb

In the late 1940's, Hawai'i Volcanoes National Park rangers had no inkling of the consequences their clever invention of "Pele's Curse" might have. Russ Apple, a former ranger, explained, "The object of 'Pele's Curse' was to convince visitors that if they took anything (from the park), they would have bad luck, and it worked. The intention of the rangers and naturalists at Volcanoes National Park in starting and promoting the story of 'Pele's curse' was to protect the park's natural environment, which includes rock-strewn landscapes. If everyone took stones, it would be barren of the rocks that Pele has spewed out of the volcano at different times. Also, it is against the law. Natural objects in a park must not be removed."

Unlike the proverbial rolling stone, the fanciful little tale gathered moss at every revolution, finally becoming so big and so powerful, so imbued with mana, or psychic power, that today, people around the world know of the modern urban legend and believe that it has affected their lives.

Each year, growing numbers of letters and carefully wrapped packages containing bits and pieces of lava rock arrive at park headquarters. The letters tell of unrelenting runs of bad luck, tragic accidents and sad tales of lost loves, fortunes, hopes and worse, which the writers ascribe to the fact that they took a bit of lava from the Big Island.

The growth of the legend has been phenomenal, considering that no formal effort was made to spread the word. A tour bus driver might warn his passengers, "Remember, don't take any lava. Pele gonna get you if you do." Between residents who've told visiting friends and relatives the story and journalists who have embellished and sensationalized the myth, the park today receives

The object of "Pele's curse" was to convince visitors that if they took anything, they would have bad luck, and it worked.

Russ Apple, former Park Ranger, retired Pacific Historian of National Park Service.

more returned rock than it cares to deal with. Ideally, park personnel would prefer that visitors refrain from removing natural objects from the park.

Richard Rasp, chief Park interpreter, explained, "The collector's urge that compels people to take a token remembrance is a contradiction of how we hope people will feel when they visit the park. Most national parks are considered living museums or classrooms; our park happens to be sacred ground. Taking rocks from the park is a violation of a privilege and as disrespectful as visiting a church and leaving with a piece of the wall. Attaching an evil connotation to taking the rocks seems to me, irreverent to the Hawaiian culture."

His colleague, George Frampton, Assistant Secretary for Fish and Wildlife and Parks from the U.S. Department of the Interior, said, "'Pele's curse' is a modern myth that largely diminishes the cultural significance of Pele and the associated mana that native Hawaiian tradition ascribes to the volcanic area. When the simplistic myth of a 'Pele's Curse' is perpetuated through publications and publicity which sensationalize the reported bad luck of park visitors, the efforts of the National Park Service and others to accurately portray the Hawaiian culture are hindered."

As the authors gathered information for *Powerstones*, evidence mounted illustrating that there is no basis in Hawaiian legend for the belief that bad luck will befall rock collectors. Ethnobotanist Beatrice Krauss remembered a time when no one was concerned about carrying lava inter-island. She said, "This 'Pele's curse' is a more recent thing. It's been around, I would say, not more than 20 years. Well I'm 92 and when you get older you think time is shorter than it really is, so maybe it's 30 or 40 years at the most. When I was a child, everybody took a piece of lava as a keepsake,

When I was a child, everybody took a piece of lava as a keepsake, but the favorite thing to do was to put a penny on the end of a stick, carefully dip it into red hot lava and bring it back as a souvenir. Everyone did it. There was never a question that one would suffer for having taken it.

Beatrice Krauss, Ethnobotanist.

but the favorite thing to do was to put a penny on the end of a stick, carefully dip it into red hot lava and bring it back as a souvenir. Everyone did it. There was never a question one would suffer for having taken it."

On the other hand, in the planning of this book, it became apparent there is most certainly a basis in the Hawaiian culture for a reverence toward pōhaku, stones. From the very beginning of habitation in Hawai'i, perhaps 1,200 years ago or more, stones were part of the foundation of Hawaiian life. Legends say that when Polynesians sailed from the Marquesas and Tahiti, they brought sacred stones to place in the bases of Hawai'i's first heiau, stone temples. Built overlooking the sea, the heiau were thought to maintain an invisible link with the motherland. As in many cultures throughout the world, stones were important not only for their everyday uses—adzes, 'ili 'ili (music makers), cooking, building blocks in roads and houses, and games (kōnane, 'ulu maika)—but also for their religious significance. A single stone monument, a Pōhaku o Kane, was placed on a small rock altar surrounded by ti leaves, which was regarded as a place of refuge as well as a gateway to heaven. Men in the family came to this sacred place to ask the gods for blessings or for forgiveness for such lapses as being irreverent. Some stones were used by the kahuna for divination; other flat stones might be put under a person's pillow to keep his spirit from wandering.

Stones were important in the women's world, as well. Great birthing stones that supported chiefly mothers in a semi-sitting position still exist in Wahiawā on O'ahu and at Wailua on Kaua'i. When a Hawaiian noble woman gave birth among sanctified clusters of rocks, mana was con-

Taking rocks from the park is a violation of a privilege and as disrespectful as visiting a church and leaving with a piece of the wall. Attaching an evil connotation to taking the rocks seems to me, irreverent to the Hawaiian culture.

Richard Rasp, Chief Park Interpreter.

veyed to the newborn. Tradition decreed that a child born of a mother who laid properly on the stones would be a child born with honor. The child would be called a chief divine.

The in-dwelling spirits of rocks have been known in many traditional cultures of the world and among most Pacific Island groups. The headhunters of Borneo, the mountain people of the Philippines and the tribal people of India believed in the power of stones as places where spirits resided. Even American Indians venerate sacred rocks and stones. The Crow Indians keep small, animal-shaped stones as powerful medicine. The Pueblo Indians believe that a hunter's good luck depends on his possession of stones of an unusual shape.

Still today, many Hawaiians believe stones, like all things in the universe, have an element of power and life beyond the obvious. Some stones are inhabited by spirits, some have mana. Belief in the power of stones continues among many modern peoples of the world. Gemstones, perhaps because of their beauty and relative value, often are thought to hold unexplainable powers. The Hope Diamond is a notorious example of a stone with powerful mana. Disasters, including deaths from suicide, shooting, hanging and auto accidents, seem to have befallen nearly every owner of the blue-violet stone since Marie Antoinette wore it. On a more inspirational note, many thoroughly modern people of all nationalities swear by the healing power of crystals, and wear or carry a stone or two on their person at all times.

Considering the nearly universal attitude of reverence toward rocks, it is easy to understand why Pele's curse was so eagerly accepted by the world at large, and why Pele was the perfect goddess to carry responsibility for dispensing bad luck. Terence Barrow, Ph.D. wrote, "Stories of

There is no curse, but there is an essence of some kind in the rocks. Positive and negative exist in all things. If you give something positive energy and use it for good, you create good. If you treat it as an object of reverence and education, this is what you will receive back.

Nalani Kanakaole, Kumu Hula, Caretaker of Pele chants.

Pele's curses are among the most dramatic in Hawaiian tradition. In Hawai'i, she became preeminent as a volcano-fire akua wahine, female deity. She is a goddess with sisters who like herself are devoted to sorcery."

Pele was traditionally associated with the volcano area, with being revengeful, with acting on capricious whims. She was the ideal figure to dispense bad luck to those who displeased her by taking away her possessions. After all, Pele was used to having sacrifices made to her—ohelo berries, pigs, etc. She wasn't used to having things taken away. Belief in Pele continues to run strong and deep. Nalani Kanakaole, a kumu hula who safeguards the chants of Pele, said, "I watched a ceremony that ended the threatening eruption of the '70s. A pig offered with prayers to Pele ran directly to a flowing lava stream. The molten lava consumed the pig in acceptance of the offering. Then, the flow stopped. People in Puna can stop this current eruption anytime they want, but they won't go back to the old ways."

Kanakaole continued, "There is no curse, but there is an essence of some kind in the rocks. Positive and negative exist in all things. If you give something positive energy and use it for good, you create good. If you treat it as an object of reverence and education, this is what you will receive back."

Years of study have also convinced Dr. Barrow of the power of mental projection as exercised by many early Hawaiians. He wrote, "After half a century of scholarly research and investigation and being associated with Polynesian cultures, I believe quite firmly the mind has the power of focusing to a point of projecting good or evil on another human. Stones have been effective

After half a century of scholarly research and investigation, and being associated with Polynesian cultures, I believe quite firmly the mind has the power of focusing to a point of projecting good or evil on another human. Stones have been effective mediums for some practitioners or priests in accumulating and conveying such energy.

Doctor Terence Barrow, Ph.D., Ethnologist, Anthropologist.

mediums for some practitioners or priests in accumulating and conveying such energy." In contemplating the easy acceptance worldwide that bad luck can result from merely moving an object of nature and the growth of this urban myth which had no real basis in Hawaiian legend, it becomes apparent that ultimately the mind is perhaps the most powerful entity of all.

Modern physics may prove what the Hawaiians knew all along—there is an energy or life force in all objects and beings. Our own investigative journey has taken us from considering the beliefs of the Hawaiian culture, to wondering at a tale that spread worldwide and resulted in thousands of soul-searching letters. Upon uncovering the hoax of Pele's Curse, we re-examined the premise of our book, which was to simply reprint the letters. There was now a larger story. We wanted to investigate the nature of belief.

On the final pages of *Powerstones,* we have interviewed leading power thinkers, truth seekers and magic makers of our time—people whose own lives illustrate how beliefs can become realities. We've questioned them on the phenomenon of Pele's Curse. Do beliefs become self-fulfilling prophesies? As Hawaiians project spirit and energy into sacred rocks, do respected power thinkers project their own will to succeed—to find truth—to make magic in the world around them? In research labs throughout the world, data is emerging which shows that human potential is far vaster than ever imagined. The potential of the human being as we move toward the 21st century is mysterious, miraculous and quite possibly limitless.

Perhaps the real gift of the myth of Pele's Curse has been to make us question what we choose to believe. It illustrates the power of belief in shaping our perceptions, our dreams and our lives.

*Wise men, theological sages,
keepers of wisdom,
lives invested in seeking
the truth, help us to
understand the power
of our beliefs.*

Truth Seekers

The Power of Beliefs

"Whatsoever a man thinketh or believeth in his heart, so is he."

I think a book like this is very important. It can bring enlightenment and freedom from darkness to people who have been concerned about this matter of the rocks. During my years of service, not just at Kawaiahao Church but in my 52 years in the ministry, many people have come to see me regarding the rocks. They thought their bad luck was caused by the rocks they took from different areas of the Hawaiian Islands including Hawai'i Volcanoes National Park. They felt they were marked, like the mark of Cain, with bad luck following them wherever they went. I would tell them, "every form of life has the imprint or signature of its creator— every fish, bird, animal, every rock." Rocks are God's material for making earth. They are God's building blocks. Eventually they become the source of life for plants, the soil in which we plant seeds. In seeing the whole plan of the Creator, many felt relieved and realized that the rocks are neutral. However, others were still convinced that there was evil in the rocks and said, "If I get rid of this rock, it will get rid of the evil." What people believe in is what becomes true. The Bible says it well, "Whatsoever man thinketh or believeth in his heart, so is he."

Man is the "crown of God's creation" because his mind can go up beyond the stars and down to the smallest atom. Like no other creature, he can contemplate the future and the past as well. I think all things in nature also have within them an identity, a structure, a place and a meaning. In God's way of doing things, everything belongs exactly where He put it. Take a look around you and enjoy what God has given you. Leave things where they should be. Be respectful. Be responsible.

*"I give you this earth.
If you take care of it,
it will take care of you."*

Rev. Abraham Akaka

Hawai'i's revered spiritual leader was a Living Treasure, beloved and respected by all.

"We are part of nature and the environment, not above it. Cause and effect is undeniable in nature and in human life—what you reap is what you sow. If you wish to harvest in the fall, you must plant in the spring. Good fortune comes from good deeds. We, therefore, need to take care of our planet as our only home and as our Mother Earth."

The Dalai Lama
His Holiness Tenzin Gyatso
—the 14th Dalai Lama,
reincarnation of the
Buddha of Compassion,
head of state for Tibetan
government-in-exile, and
winner of the 1989 Nobel
Peace Prize.

If we create our own reality, how would you explain the thousands of letters from those who say they did not believe in the curse until their lives were severely impacted by it?

"The weak meaning of a statement like 'We create our own reality' is that the way we perceive the world around us (and ourselves) is affected by the contents of our unconscious minds. The stronger meaning is that we are indeed co-creators of that world and that ultimate cause of any phenomenon is to be sought not in the physical, but in consciousness."

The belief in "Pele's Curse" would not be a great surprise to someone who believed in Carl Jung's concept of synchronicity. Jung suggested that synchronicity may be regarded in the same fundamental dimension of objective reality as space, time and energy. He viewed everything as being connected, not only in the physical sense but also by a web of meaning. When we attach meaning to a belief such as "Pele's curse," it would have power, no matter how recently it was created. When people come to believe it, the whole world would shift in terms of that new belief. Now, since this does not make any sense in the terms of the worldview of Western science, one would have to conclude that there was something faulty about the worldview of Western science or that there is nothing to synchronicity. While Western science does very well with the ob-

Willis Harman, Ph.D.

President, Institute of Noetic Sciences,
Regent, University of California, 1980–1990;
author of *Global Mind Change, An
Incomplete Guide to the Future, Creative
Work.* Willis W. Harman obtained his
doctorate in electrical engineering and
taught at University of Florida and Stanford
Universities. In 1966 he was appointed
director for the Center for the Study of Social
Policy at the Stanford Research Institute
(presently SRI International).

jective world we perceive with our senses, it doesn't do well with the subjective experiences of our consciousness.

If you look at traditional spiritual understandings of the East (and also elsewhere in the world), the most fundamental aspect of reality in their philosophical wisdom is that ultimate cause is subjective and effect is objective. That is ultimately, our minds are all part of a universal mind and ideas of separateness are illusory. It would follow that the Eastern mind would respond to the concept of synchronicity with, "Of course," and the Western mind would say, "Big surprise," because ideas of synchronicity do not go with Western scientific laws. Maybe it's time to reevaluate these laws.

The world is undergoing a revolutionary transformation more radical than any since the scientific revolution. There is a "global mind change" that is shifting from a worldview that sees physical reality as primary, to one that sees the mind as primary. It acknowledges that the mind gives rise to physical reality. The gut beliefs of people living in industrial societies have been changing in the last fifteen years. And there had not been a comparable change on the same level of profundity since the time of Copernicus. It is difficult to recognize revolution in the midst of its evolvement. Could we have perceived, in the middle of the seventeenth century, that from the ideas of Copernicus and Galileo would emerge a conceptual revolution that would eventually shake society to its very roots? We could have imagined these new ideas about the planets as being of great interest to theologians and philosophers, but they could hardly have been expected to make much impact on the physical world of everyday experience. And yet, as we all know, they did in time affect every institution in society.

Most of us have been inclined to leave basic issues of scientific methodology to scientists. But when these issues become matters which obviously affect our lives, they become issues of public concern. These concerns act as an impetus for change. I would describe the most essential features of this shift in worldview as:

1) Increased emphasis on interconnectedness and recognition that external and internal are only different aspects of the same oneness (particularly visible in the "deep ecology" and feminist-spiritual movements).

2) A shift in the focus of authority from external to internal. Whether in religion, politics, or science, we see growing disenchantment with external authorities and increasing reliance on intuitive inner wisdom and authority (apparent in transpersonal psychology, the feminist movement, psychotherapy, and executive training, and in the assumption of inner divinity in the "new spirituality").

3) A shift in the perception of cause from external to internal. The weak meaning of a statement like "We create our own reality" is that the way we perceive the world around us (and ourselves) is affected by the contents of our unconscious and preconscious minds. The stronger meaning is that we are indeed co-creators of that world and that ultimate cause of any phenomenon is to be sought not in the physical, but in consciousness.

Rubellite Johnson

Author, speaker, Pacific representative
to the Global Forum, Environment and
Survival, Moscow, Professor; Hawaiian
Language/Literature, University of Hawaii–
Manoa, recently retired. Her masterwork
is the on-going study and translation of
the *Kumulipo* (The Hawiian Chant of
Creation) with a focus on Ethnoastronomy.

You are considered Hawai'i's foremost scholar on Hawaiian mythology and a valued resource for cultural reference. Do the Hawaiian spiritual beliefs attribute a powerful element to Pele's rocks?

"The idea of rocks having negative effects has built up from years of story telling but its roots is in this fundamental, universal principle— it is wrong to desecrate the land."

It has become convenient to call the power of these stones "Pele's Curse" but the belief is not limited to stones or to the association of Pele. It is actually part of a bigger belief in "residual mana." Hawaiian societies made a clear distinction between living and non-living matter, the animate and inanimate but whatever the classification, they believed all things could be "pregnant" with mana— the life force, a source of divine vitality.

The idea of the rocks having negative effects has built up from years of story telling but its root is in this fundamental universal principle—it is wrong to desecrate the land.

There is a tendency today to make mana exclusive to Hawaiians. It is not. It is not Polynesian thought to limit mana within ethnic boundaries. We know that the universality of mana is applicable beyond one's ethnicity for it is not part of the essential ethnic make up of a people but rather the ancestral pattern of history that was carried with them throughout their migration. The creator is not limited by race. Power, creation, and spirituality are not bound by place. In the same way "residual mana" is also universal.

What guidance would I give someone fearful of "Pele's Curse"? I'm an American so I try to observe this culture, but family is of Pele lineage. The genealogy traces back to Borabora. My name Kawena comes from the Pele tradition and translates as "a shadow profile against the red glow." This refers to the after glow of an eruption and reminder that all Pele's sisters remained in the shadows behind the Goddess. My grandmother practiced the old ways. She honored a special stone which was called, "The Woman of Ni'ihau." It sat on a shrine in the middle of her house looking out over the garden. Everyday tutu would adorn the "Woman From Ni'ihau" with maunaloa leis which she strung out of blossoms from her garden. This was one of the ways she paid homage to it. People today may feel discomfort, because they don't know how to function around these old religious or spiritual rules so they nervously send the rocks back.

If you took a stone, perhaps unknowingly or without meaning disrespect, I would recommend a ceremony rather then sending the rocks back. Say, "Release me from this kapu. I *oki* (end) this." Just let it go.

Dr. Aoki, you have been a healer and a comfort for so many people. What would you say to those who fear "Pele's Curse"?

"The letters sent to the Park from believers of "Pele's Curse" resonate with guilt. The deeper the guilt, the more awesome the consequences."

I would ask them, "What would Madame Pele think about the thousands of rocks returned to the park?" I think she would be having a good laugh about it.

The letters sent to the Park from the believers of "Pele's Curse" resonate with guilt. The deeper the guilt, the more awesome the consequences. Negative emotions impact our minds and bodies and influence our lives. However, in my involvement with over 600 cancer patients, I've seen remarkable results and remissions in those who committed fully to the application of holistic health concepts.

The power of love and positive emotions has been demonstrated in many scientific studies. A Harvard University based experiment referred to as "The Mother Theresa Effect" was conducted by David McClelland, Ph.D. He showed students a documentary on Mother Theresa caring for patients in India. They were tested before and after the film for an antibody active against viral infections. The post-film testing revealed the immune system had been enhanced and strengthened significantly. McClelland demonstrated the same results when students imagined feeling loved or deeply loving another person. The mind is a powerful tool in supporting the health of the body.

In another experiment, Psychologist G. Frank Lawlis and psychophysiologist Jeanne Achterberg researched the effect of creative visualization on 126 cancer patients. Under hypnosis, patients imagined their white blood cells as sharks feeding on the cancer cells and destroying them. These investigators found a positive correlation between the use of visualization and future tumor growth and remission in these patients.

We're on the edge of a revolution in medicine and healing. If we can help the body cope with serious illness, we can certainly cure the mind of fear and guilt. To those who have taken rocks and still feel uneasy, I would say ask for forgiveness and receive the blessing of Pele.

Dr. Mitsuo Aoki,

Doctor of Divinity, Pacific School
of Religion, Past Chairman of
the Department of Religion,
University of Hawai'i. Dr. Aoki,
President of The Foundation for
Holistic Healing lives in Honolulu,
Hawai'i. He applies holistic
principles in workshops on
Death and Dying and lectures
on Wellness and Healing.

*Philosophers, scientists,
caretakers of the body, mind,
and soul, dedicated to expanding
the human potential and exploring
the unlimited possibilities of
human life, give us insight into
understanding our beliefs and
how they impact our lives.*

Power Thinkers

We Are Empowered

If beliefs become our realities, how would you explain the thousands of letters from people who say they did not believe in "Pele's Curse" until their lives were severely impacted by it?

The human mind is a field of information and energy that is made up of air, fire, water, and space. Like everything else, it is a part of a larger field of information and energy. Therefore, you can say that the human mind is a localized concentration of a larger mind that exists in nature. Nature thinks, and by this I mean it thinks in the form of information and energy. If our mind introduces a certain impulse of information and energy, it alters the total field however miniscule that alteration may be. There are studies that show that a butterfly can flap its wings in Texas and you can get a tornado in Massachusetts if the disturbance is at some critical concentration of energy and information. Similarly, if you have turbulence in your mind it will affect the field however miniscule that effect might be.

Is it an electrical impulse?

It is information, which is more subtle than electromagnetic energy. Einstein said energy and matter are the same but he didn't tell us about the next step. The next step is that every field of energy has an informational content. When you switch on your television, for example, you are capturing electromagnetic energy. The difference between the programs you are watching is not the electromagnetic field but the informational content and how it is arranged. When this energy is released into the universe it is neither lost nor destroyed. It is always with us. Believing in the curse changes the informational content of the field, affecting those who adopt it into their belief system. Turbulence can be caused by the collective mind and the collective mind is information.

"Turbulence can be caused by the collective mind and the collective mind is information."

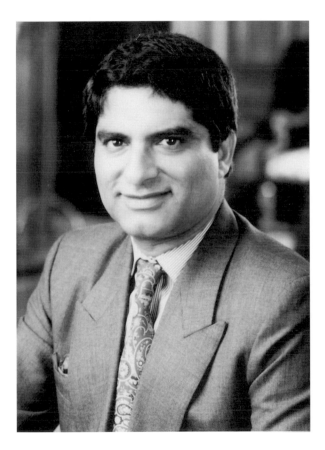

Deepak Chopra, M.D.

Author, *Ageless Body, Timeless Mind*, and *Quantum Healing*. Groundbreaking pioneer in the field of mind-body medicine and human potential.

Our research into ancient Hawaiian folklore does not substantiate a basis for the belief in "Pele's Curse." However, a growing number of testimonial letters suggest otherwise. Can you provide insight into the meaning of this phenomena?

"Pele is the symbol of the death and resurrection that we experience every day. As we sit and feast our eyes and celebrate the magnificence of her domain, we must realize the need to stop the conspicuous consumption of the outer world."

The phenomena of Pele's Curse is an example of something that was started as a ruse to keep people from taking rocks, but the ruse became mythic. It became storied and it became a myth. With the affirmation of thousands of people yearly and perhaps hundreds of thousands over the decades, it entered into the realm of the collective unconscious.

People come to this paradise called Hawai'i that is filled with prodigious natural wonders. They see people performing extraordinary chants and dances, and they become immersed in a dynamic living culture. They are told the dark side story of Madame Pele. This story is held in the shadows of the culture. It attracts other shadows and fears from the stories of their own lives. It creates a constellation of fearful or shadowed energy. The adrenalin rises, which gives the myth further energy, and one builds up a whole resonance of expectations. Thoughts are things, they are energy, vibrations, and frequencies. Scientists are just at the beginning of understanding the frequency domain as it applies to psychology. Unfortunately, we are twenty to thirty years away from understanding the physic neurobiology of the psyche.

The psyche of the 21st century is going to look very different than it does today. The

Dr. Jean Houston

Psychologist, scholar, philosopher, teacher, and author of numerous books, including *The Possible Human, The Search for the Beloved, The Hero and The Goddess,* and *Public Like a Frog.* This year she received the Gardner Murphy Award in Science, the INTA Award as Humanitarian of the Year, as well as the Lifetime Creative Achievement Award.

sheer complexity of modern life has given many of us five to a hundred times the amount of experience of our ancestors of a hundred years ago. We require many different persona and frames of mind to deal with all this experience. And with so much more experience, we often end up more psychologically wounded than our ancestors.

Every great story, every great myth has wounding at its center. Christ must have His Crucifixion. Artemis must kill him who comes too close. Persephone must be taken down and married to darkness. The wounding tends to open you to be vulnerable and available to others as you never have been before. This can result in compassion and expansion of the heart. The traumatic events occurring to those after taking the lava rocks have greatly added to their capacity for compassion and empathy.

We are moving to a planetary society. We are being linked via our media as we never have been before. We watch television and see horrors, violence, and massive disasters on an international plane. We see the breakdown in the belief in people we thought were great heroes. We are in a time where everything is breaking down. However, in the dissolution is the basis for reconstruction. We are understanding human capacities as we never have before. Women are rising up to full partnership with men in the whole domain of human affairs.

This is "jump time." A time when we become responsible for planetary governments, making the planet work for everyone. You don't become responsible until you've had a lot of experience, and people are having their human experience accelerated so as to prepare for the depth and breadth of "jump time."

This planet is requiring us to go to our edges to continue to grow, to be worthy stewards of a whole evolutionary process. In the taking of the lava rocks, people have greatly added to their own story. Through the traumatic events, they have acquired a wealth of experience. They took on a larger story. They grew their souls.

I have a fascinating story to tell. It was told to me by a person not given to telling tall tales. He knew a young Filipino couple who lived in Hawai'i, whose happiness was marred by the fact that, although they had been married for five years, the wife could not get pregnant. The man was also bored with his job. While driving on the Big Island during a massive rain storm, he saw a beautiful woman. She was dressed in white and walking on the road. He stopped the car and offered her a ride. "Please get in and I will take you wherever you need to go."

Strangely, she was completely dry and was wearing a crown of flowers. She said, "No, I am fine. But would you make a phone call for me? Please remember this number and tell the people you saw me. They'll know what that means." He drove away, but then turned back, worried about her. She was gone! He made the phone call for her and was asked, "Do you know who that was? It was Madame Pele. We are kahunas and we know what she wants." He was then asked, "Did you offer her a ride?" And he answered, "Yes." "Good thing that you did!" was their reply. This man went on to have many children and found a job that he loved as a welder. Interesting, isn't it? He ended up working with fire.

Many of these encounters with Madam Pele have been documented and permeate the culture. The evidence of her spirit is so commanding, it is no wonder we feel her essence moving among us.

Madame Pele has been given "bad press" as being a tempestuous goddess of upset and destruction. However, she is also a goddess of creation, wonder, and astonishment. Would you please comment?

Madame Pele is a Being of extraordinary fruitfulness, and of power. She is a goddess who says, "Don't be small and mean-heart-ed." She is the fire that burns the old toxins within us so that we can be renewed. Pele is the symbol of the death and resurrection that we experience every day. As we sit and feast our eyes and celebrate the magnificence of her domain, we must realize the need to stop the conspicuous consumption of the outer world. If people were to take a souvenir from Hawai'i Volcanoes National Park, I think they can take a souvenir of "ebullience in the bones," of a tremendous sense of the dynamic spirit of life that is there. The joy of it, the juiciness of it, the great hot magma of new life forming, creating, and re-creating in their hearts, in their minds, and in their bones. What a grand souvenir to take home!

When we are in a weakened state of fear, helplessness, guilt or confusion, can we draw negative energy from the "collective unconscious"?

You link the negative energies to being in a specific "state," and I think that's a key to the phenomenon. Some of the most extraordinary breakthroughs of the current scientific brain revolution involve surprising insights into the powerful connection between state —immaterial, intangible, seemingly elusive and transitory states of consciousness, states of mind, states of being—and the hard material reality of our bodies and brains and the events of our external world. One example of this connection is the field of psychoneuroimmunology—the discovery that mind states can have dramatic effects on the immune system.

In investigating this link scientists have discovered the phenomenon of state dependency. Memories, for example, are state dependent, in that we can remember things better when we are in the state we were in when the memories were first laid down. According to Dr. Gordon Power, of Stanford University, one of the pioneer explorers of state dependent memory, states are like "different libraries into which a person places memory records. A given memory record can be retrieved only by returning into that library…" That is, as scientists have proven in numerous rigorous studies, what we have learned or experienced when we are sad is best remembered later when we are sad; what we experienced in anger is best remembered in anger; our most joyous past moments are most fully recalled in present states of joy.

While interesting in itself, this insight provides us with a new view of states as not merely passive situations or ways of being, but dynamic and powerful active forces. That is, to look at state dependency in another way, our present state acts like a powerful magnet to memories or past experiences that are linked to that state. When you're sad, you tend to attract sad memories, recollections and associations.

As various poets and philosophers have observed, our minds can make of the vast world a prison cell, or can turn a prison cell into an eternity of delight. Our reality, as the scientific evidence has proven, is largely a product of our state.

How is it that thousands of seemingly well-educated, rational humans can become victims to this belief?

The one thing they all have in common is that they travelled to Hawai'i. Virtually all of them came as tourists or travellers. By definition, travellers and tourists are in a heightened state of consciousness—they are ready for something wholly different from their ordinary life or reality. Their senses are heightened and intensified, they are open to change, to new insights, to new beliefs. And of course, travelling to Hawai'i is quite different from a trip to Disney World or the golf course. In Hawai'i, the natural beauty is exhilarating, powerful, sublime, but also alien, other-worldly in many ways—such as in the lunar landscapes of volcanic rock sweeping down to the sea, or in the churning cauldrons of the volcanic depths. So, not only are visitors in a heightened, receptive state, they are also presented with intense, ineffable experiences of the inhuman power and turbulent beauty of the natural world. That is, they are in a heightened state that is ideal for the implantation of new beliefs. In this case, the belief is one in which the awesome spectacle of natural beauty and power becomes embodied in the persona and the curse of Pele.

It says something important about contemporary culture that we are so open to beliefs having to do with fear, tragedy, and the alien power of The Other, or nature. Having largely suppressed the power of nature and The Other within ourselves, and having actively destroyed and "tamed" the wilderness (and wildness) of the planet and the powers of nature with our own civilization, it makes sense that this power would re-emerge in other forms, ranging from nightmares to our personal and cultural demons, addictions, tragedies, and woes.

Michael Hutchison

Award-winning writer. Author of
Megabrain, The Book of Floating
and *The Anatomy of Sex and Power:
An Investigation of Mind-Body Politics.*
On the cutting edge of applying high
technology to attaining peak performance.

It is believed that misfortune follows those who take rocks from Pele's domain at the Hawai'i Volcanoes National Park. She is the goddess of Fire and this belief is often referred to as "Pele's Curse." Our research in Hawaiian mythology does not substantiate a basis for this curse; however, a ton of rocks are returned to the park each year with a growing number of letters testifying to the contrary. We have, in fact, discovered that the story of the curse is fictitious and made up in the late 40's or early 50's. How would you explain this phenomenon based on your research and studies?

There are studies which show that intermediary substances, like rocks, can catalyze events when they are placed in the vicinity of living things. We also know, for example, that the water at Lourdes, France, is said to have healing effects and the same belief is attached to the soil of a sacred sanctuary in northern New Mexico. From a scientific point of view, carefully documented experiments by Dr. Bernard Grad at McGill University in Canada illustrate how intermediary substances can cause physical change. Dr. Grad tested a healer's claim that healing effects could be transmitted by secondary materials. A piece of cotton wool was placed in the healer's hand, then put into test animals' cages. These animals, exposed to the cotton wool, healed significantly faster when compared to the control group. In this instance, an intermediary substance was able, apparently, to catalyze something positively. But I think we have to put the possibility on the table that there is a flip side to that. There may be something related to the rocks that can bring about negative changes in people's lives. If a person in possession of the rock believes that it has some sort of negative effect, this can be very powerful and, in this sense, it wouldn't matter what the creators of the curse said or what is said now.

We know it is possible to achieve negative effects in the laboratory from a distance. Studies provide abundant evidence that positive prayer, even from a distance, can accelerate the growth of lower organisms such as fungi, yeast, bacteria, and germinating seeds. The opposite also holds true. Negative prayer can inhibit their growth and have harmful effects. We cannot dismiss these outcomes as being due to the power of suggestion since these lower organisms do not think in any conventional sense and therefore are not susceptible to the power of suggestion.

What I'm suggesting is that belief, although extraordinary and powerful, certainly is not everything. It is arrogant to say that we created all consciously, or that our beliefs structure everything. Science always raises more mysteries and questions than it answers. I believe it's much more honest to acknowledge the great unknown and honor the mystery. It's much more majestic and fulfilling to say that in spite of the fact that we don't know all of the mysterious happenings of the universe, it still works in the most glorious and benevolent ways.

"It is arrogant to say that we created all consciously, or that our beliefs structure everything. …It's much more honest to acknowledge the great unknown and honor the mystery."

Larry Dossey, M.D.

Author of *Healing Words, Space, Time & Medicine, Beyond Illness, Recovering the Soul,* and *Meaning & Medicine.* Former Chief of Staff of Humana Medical City, Dallas. Co-chairman of the Panel on Mind/Body Interventions, Office of Alternative Medicine, Nat'l Institutes of Health.

What would you say to believers of "Pele's Curse"?

"Take the hit as a gift..."

My friend George Leonard developed a set of exercises that dramatize life's challenges and lessons. In theory, you take a blow, bend with it, turn the momentum back to the attacker, and turn the fight into a dance. With each blow comes energy. This energy is a gift. Feel it, use it, then transcend it by saying, "I am beyond it, I am stronger for it, I will take this energy to enrich my life." In the same way, we can take the blow of this fake curse and use it to examine our own susceptibilities, our propensity to be made a victim, or we can use it for the adventure it provides.

Quantum physics has given us evidence that the particles which make up an atom have a degree of freedom. Scientists now say every law has "wiggle room." Philosopher Alfred North Whitehead said, "laws are really habits" because they can change at different points in the unfoldment of the universe. We can see, then, that not only do all objects have energy, but also degrees of freedom. Furthermore, there is evidence each object has some sort of subjectivity or soul in it. Parapsychology studies show that objects will respond to human attention. This is also a belief found in the common lore of every nation since the beginning of recorded history. Our ancestors thought that all objects were alive. In modern times we have denied this and now we see the consequences. If we approach all things in a loving way, we will experience that love returned. In a sense, everything is wanting to be touched, wanting to be next, wanting to be loved. Everything gives back love in its own way. So I would say love the rock and dissolve the curse. Every object in nature is a potential lover.

Michael Murphy

Visionary writer, co-founder of Esalen Institute, Author, *Golf in the Kingdom, Future of the Body,* and co-author, with George Leonard, *The Life We are Given.*

What message do you see in the letters?

"The curse is not the power, it is the belief we hold that affects us so strongly."

One wonders if the story concerning the curse of the lava stones is made up or not. Let's use our imagination to look beyond these letters and ask ourselves another question. What happened to the many people, including those unaware of the curse, who picked up the rocks and, in that aloha moment, decided to honor nature and leave the rocks where they found them? If we believe that the curse is true—that "bad" things happened to people who took the rocks away—then perhaps the opposite is also true—good things happened to those who didn't. The opposite would bring magic and miracles.

There is power in the moment of making a decision, not based on fear, but rather, out of wanting to honor a place with the spirit of aloha. The real message of the letters, I believe, is that it's always better to honor a place with aloha. This is true today as it was in the 50's when, I understand, the story was made up to discourage people from taking rocks away.

Whether we believe this curse (or any curse) or choose a better belief such as, honoring a place because it is the right thing to do, it becomes the paradigm which limits or motivates us. Fear constricts us, aloha expands us. The curse is not the power, it's the belief we hold that affects us so strongly.

Spencer Johnson, M.D.

Co-Author *The One Minute Manager*
As a result of successfully making his
dream a reality, Dr. Johnson resides in
Hawai'i with his wife and family. He draws
inspiration daily from his own back yard
…the breathtaking Pacific Ocean.

Artists, athletes, writers,
all commanding our attention,
lives in search of excellence,
following their own truths,
provide us inspiration for
making beliefs into realities.

Magic Makers

Making It Happen

"Come clad in peace,
And I will sing the songs
The Creator gave to me when I and the
Tree and the Rock were one…"

Maya Angelou
On the Pulse of Morning

Maya Angelou

Author of *I Know Why the*
Caged Bird Sings, I Shall Not
Be Moved, Heat of A Woman.
She moved and inspired the
nation with her Inaugural poem,
On the Pulse of Morning.
Maya Angelou is currently Reynold
Professor at Wake Forest University,
North Carolina.

Would you address the fears of those who believe in "Pele's Curse"?

"You create your life with your words and they in turn create you."

In all the great religious traditions; Judeo-Christian, Buddhism, Zen, and others, there is a statement or suggestion that, "in the beginning was the word...."

I know words are things. So one must be careful about the words one uses. You create your life with your words, and they in turn create you.

When you really want something, tell it to Energy and to yourself. "I really want...." When I was young, I wanted a job on the municipal railway. The conductors looked so snappy...caps with brims, shiny uniforms, money changer. I went to apply for the job, but the secretaries wouldn't give me an application. I returned home crushed. My mother asked, "Do you know why?" "Uh huh, because I'm a Negro." "But do you want that job? Do you really want that job?" "I really want it." "Then go there before the secretaries come in and when they enter, you go in and sit there. Take a good book.

At lunch don't leave until the secretaries have left and you return before they return ...if you want it." I said, "I *want* it."

By the third day I hated it. The women would step all over me and they were rude. They all but spat on me. But I sat, patiently waiting to be given an application. I was fifteen and I had said I wanted that job. I told my mother I wanted it, and I decided yes, I wanted it. It took one month of this painful daily routine, but I got the job. The newspaper reported, "First Negro to work on the streetcars...."

When you want something as much as a drowning man wants air then you'll find it. You must want it, and in the wanting there is a building up of your persona, your spirit.

When fear, guilt or trepidation visit me, I speak out loud, "I am a child of God, of good." I want that, I know that, I claim that, and I have that, Thank God.

You have been a champion and a role model for decades. Your name is synonymous with excellence and endurance. As one whose life has been an inspiration to others, where do you draw your strength to face life's challenges?

For all my life, as far back as I can remember, I've been very self-disciplined. My parent's passion for excellence fueled my drive to constantly strive for a higher standard in life. Not only in golf and business, but within my personal life as well. My father was truly a task master, a real tough guy. My mother taught me to appreciate the gentler side of life, and I am blessed with gifts from each of them. Both preached the meaning of respect for others, a strong belief in God and country, but most of all, humility. They were my teachers and role models.

With this strong influence, I have enjoyed over forty years of competitive tournament golf. During this time I have met literally millions of golf fans who have always treated me with respect while I played this great game. In fact, some people have called these fans, "Arnie's Army." I often reflect on how both my parents' strong influence and the public's belief in me provided the strength and inspiration needed to overcome adversity and to prevail in the game of golf, in business and in life.

Arnold Palmer

Championship professional golfer
entrepreneur, international
ambassador of goodwill. "Arnie"
is credited with the popularity
of the modern PGA tour and the
Senior Tour. Having won the Masters,
the U.S. Open, the British Open and
over 60 tournaments, Arnie is known
in golfing circles as "The King."

"Thought is everything. We are ceaselessly sending our words afloat on the great ocean of life. Every thought is creative. As an artist and a woman, I know this to be true. Our declarations come back to us and mold our daily lives. So to the believers of Pele's curse, I say, watch your words well.

My recipe for happiness? Eat dessert first...preferably chocolate."

Beatrice Wood

Artist, and a lover of life.
Known as the Mama of
the Dada art movement.
At 101 years old, Beatrice has
mastered the fine art of living.
Author of *I Shock Myself*. She
is a scintillating conversationalist
and a connoisseur of chocolate.

The story of "Pele's Curse" is truly a metaphor for addressing one's fears and liberating one from a sense of victimization. From where do you draw your strength to creatively face life's challenges? Would you please give examples from your own life?

"From day one I was told my genetic pattern was to have a bold spirit, and to create a world that enabled the spirit to flourish."

The landscapes, peoples, and experiences that have shaped me are kept alive in my soul through the stories attached to them. I am the sum total of these stories and experiences. The places, events, and people that we know make their mark on us like the curves and dots of some inward map which guides us through life.

My mother, for example, taught me to challenge everything. She pushed me to the edge of bravery. She challenged everything and she created a world that allowed my spirit to flourish. Every time I did anything kind or loving to anyone, she would delight in it. From day one I was told my genetic pattern was to have a bold spirit, and to create a world that enabled the spirit to flourish.

What words of encouragement do you have to guide and empower our readers?

I would like to share with them the words of Michael Ray and Lorna Catford, "Myths and stories are the reflection of the human soul. They remind us of our potential, of the divine possibilities of our existence." Without an awareness of your emotions you are not able to experience reverence. Reverence is not an emotion. It is a way of being, but the path to reverence is through your heart, and only an awareness of your feelings can open your heart. I'll illustrate this with a story.

Last year I spent time in, arguably, the most disadvantaged Native American Reservation, Rosebud in South Dakota. I was invited by the tribal colleges to see if I could come up with any creative solution to any one of their huge social problems. I noticed that sagebrush grew wild in the Badlands. Easy, I thought. Gather the sagebush, extract the essential oil, and convert it into personal care products. They had the plants and I had the technology. Easy. No, not easy. First, they said, we must ask for permission from the plant nation. We must do a sweat. Then, maybe.

What I learned from that experience, the ritual of the sweat lodge, was simply this. I was not on top of nature. I was part of it. It didn't teach me respect, it taught me reverence.

Anita Roddick

The Body Shop International. Forging a new face in global business with a focus on social change and consciousness. She is a recipient of the United Nations Environmentalist Award, Business Woman of the Year, Communicator of the Year, and Retailer of the Year awards.

How do you source the power of your own inner strength?

Olympia Dukakis

Academy award winning actress.

Prayer

This is the way we source the power of the Goddess.

Ritual

She leads us to lessons we need to learn...

Daily tasks

these experiences are not misfortunes in her eyes

Meditation

they are the paths and insights for change.

Nainoa Thompson

Navigator of twelve *Hokule'a* voyages throughout Polynesia and a teacher of Hawai'i's youth in the science of ocean exploration. He offers an understanding of this heritage with the goal of creating caretakers for the Earth's resources and its environment.

***Hokule'a* is a voyaging canoe guided by non-instrument navigation. Her first voyage in 1976 from Hawai'i to Tahiti was an odyssey many thought impossible. The journeys of *Hokule'a* are a symbol for the power of belief. What messages would you draw from these historic voyages?**

Hokule'a is driven by the beliefs of thousands of people and a million man-hours. She is a vehicle for great messages. As *Hokule'a* voyages into the 21st century, she serves as a symbol for the survival of our Earth and humanity. We will not survive without discipline, self-respect, positive beliefs, and fearless visions. These survival skills are the lessons of the teachers who guided these adventures. It would be a pleasure to grow old and see the youth influenced by *Hokule'a* become teachers themselves...teaching the excitement of life and the importance of reaching a goal or realizing a dream. Hope is a great gift. May *Hokule'a* bring the message of hope and the power of belief as we advance toward the future.

Authors' Notes

The authors wish to thank the administrators, park rangers, staff members, and volunteers at Hawai'i Volcanoes National Park for their enlightened stewardship of this sacred ground. We would also like to make a special request to our readers: If you are visiting the Park, please do not remove rocks, it is illegal and disruptive to the environment. If you have taken rocks, please do not return them. The sheer volume of rocks returned each year overburdens park personnel, whose services are needed elsewhere.

Instead, we offer up the advice of Dr. Mitsuo Aoki: "To those who have taken rocks and still feel uneasy about it, I would say, ask for forgiveness and receive the blessing of Madame Pele."

To those who feel that further amends are necessary, the authors suggest sending a donation to any one of America's national parks. Monetary contributions help support educational and environmental projects that preserve and protect these national treasures.

*As part of our ongoing research for future projects
and* Powerstones *updates, we welcome your stories on powerful stones.
We are also interested in related urban myths regarding stones.
Please write to us at the following address:*

Powerstones
55 South Kukui
Suite 1215
Honolulu, Hawaii 96813

E very book is a collaborative effort.
Ours is not an exception. We would like to thank the fine
photographers who's works grace the pages of *Powerstones*.

Thank you to all who contributed much in
countless ways. We extend special thanks to:

The Estate of James Campbell
Kapiolani Health Care Systems
Hawaiian Telephone Company
Wimberly Allison Tong & Goo
Hilton Waikoloa Village
Mauna Lani Resorts, Inc.

and to these individuals for their supportive efforts,
our warmest aloha:

Governor John Waihee
Secretary Bruce Babbitt,
    US Department of the Interior
George T. Frampton, Jr.,
    Assistant Secretary for Fish and
    Wildlife and Parks
Martin Schiller, The Schiller Group
Betty Fullard-Leo
Ingelborg Ingle
Mark Otto
Andrea Cagan
Roger Jellinak
Sheila Davies
Debrah Mudd
Donna Wendt

Photo Credits